David Inglis Urquhart

THE AIRPLANE
and How It Works

Illustrated by Enrico Arno

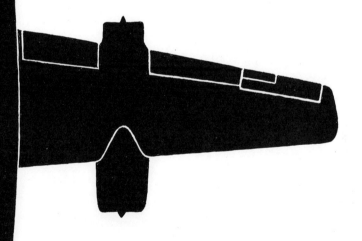

HENRY Z. WALCK, INC. · NEW YORK

Library of Congress Cataloging in Publication Data

Urquhart, David Inglis.
  The airplane and how it works.

  SUMMARY: A brief history of man's
attempts to fly accompanies a description
of the principles by which an airplane
flies.

1. Aeroplanes - Juvenile literature.
[1. Airplanes]   I. Arno, Enrico,
illus.   ◯   II. Title.
TL547.U77   629.133'34   72-10867
ISBN 0-8098-2091-9

To Jean Josie, who just had to be the first to fly.
Kuspo, Guggy and Wappage

WHEN YOU LOOK UP into the sky and see a flock of birds or a giant airplane, have you ever wondered how they can fly and you can't? At most you can jump a few feet into the air before you fall back to the ground. Man wondered about flying for thousands of years. He watched and studied the birds to try to discover their secrets. He learned a lot about flight from them and he understood much of the principles of flying long before he had the tools and materials to make a flying machine.

But what does it really mean to "fly"? Many things seem to fly through the air. When you throw a baseball or a football, they both appear to fly. But they are not flying the way an airplane or a bird flies. Both the baseball and the football are pushed or propelled by the force or energy of the athlete's arms and muscles. Flying means to travel through the air by using wings and the air itself, rather than being propelled by another force.

Do you think of a rocketship to the moon as a kind of airplane that flies? A rocketship may seem to act like an airplane but it isn't one. It does not have wings and it does not use air to stay in flight. Like a baseball propelled by a bat, the rocket is blasted into space by a powerful fuel and the fuel burns with such force that the rocketship needs no wings.

Unlike the rocketship or the balls, a balloon needs air to stay up but still it doesn't fly like a bird or an airplane. A balloon is like a boat which floats on the water while a balloon floats in the air. Years ago, scientists learned that a boat will float when it is able to displace or take the place of an amount of water equal to the weight of the boat. A balloon does the same thing with air. Balloons, blimps and dirigibles are called lighter-than-air ships, while airplanes are heavier-than-air ships. All lighter-than-air ships will rise until they reach a height at which they will displace exactly their own weight of

air. When that level is reached, the balloon, blimp or dirigible will float. The early balloons were often filled with hot air because it weighed less than regular air. When a gas, like air, is heated, it will expand or get larger in volume. Later, other gases were discovered which weighed less than air. Several of these worked well but hydrogen gas was the lightest. However, hydrogen was dangerous because it burned very easily. Today lighter-than-air ships use helium, a very light gas which will not burn. Lighter-than-air ships are still used for things like weather balloons and sport ballooning, but as a means of long-distance travel and mass transportation they were found to be too slow to be efficient.

So far the airplane has proved to be the best craft to use in the sky. It uses wings like a bird, and it depends on air to stay in flight.

Man at first tried to copy the flight of the birds. He tried to build machines with wings that he could flap. But birds have a very special quality that man and other animals don't have. Their bones are full of holes, like a sponge, which makes them very light but strong. They also have tremendously strong wing muscles which enable them to fly for hours without resting.

There are some interesting old stories about men who tried to make wings from feathers and wax. The ancient Greeks told about a man named Daedalus and his son Icarus who were

supposed to have made such wings. Icarus was too bold, and when he flew too near the sun's heat, the wax melted and his wings fell off.

Man was too heavy to fly like a bird. He could only watch the birds, and even though he gradually began to understand how birds were able to fly, it was centuries before he could develop materials light enough to build a practical plane. As long ago as the sixteenth century, the Italian painter and inventor, Leonardo da Vinci, drew plans for a plane which had wings that flapped like a bird.

Long before Leonardo the ancient Chinese experimented with putting men up into the air with kites. Some of the kites built by the Chinese were very large, and they did actually carry men up into the skies, but they could not fly from place to place. They were used as observation places from which to watch an enemy.

The first heavier-than-air craft which resembles the airplane as we know it today may have been sparked by man's knowledge of kites. This was the glider, a simple plane with a body and wings but no engine. Gliders are built of extremely light materials. A glider is so light that it can stay aloft as long as there are currents of air which will give it the lift or height it needs to fly. As gliders have no engines, they must be carried aloft by an airplane or by another force such as that supplied by a car. The glider is attached to a car by a long cable. As the car moves forward, the glider becomes airborne, just as you run with a kite to get it up in the air. When the glider is aloft, the towing cable is dropped and the glider flies on its own. It was not until the development of a power-driven aircraft that a plane could take off under its own power, but the glider's ability to stay in flight by the use of its wings and the air was a great advance for aviation. Aviation is the name given to the operation of heavier-than-air aircraft.

You have probably built model airplanes or seen someone else build them. The early inventors of the glider first worked on models.

They built their models and tested them in flight outdoors, or they built wind tunnels to learn how air could be used to make a plane fly. A wind tunnel is a tube into which air can be blown at one end, while the model of the plane is held firmly in the middle of the tube. As the air is blown past the airplane, the plane can be tested as if it were really flying. Models were very important in the whole development of airplanes. They were used as the first real proof that a heavier-than-air craft could actually fly.

Although there were a number of earlier inventors who contributed to the science of flight, credit is generally given to Otto Lilienthal as the "father" of modern aviation. In Germany, between 1891 and 1896, Otto and his brother Gustav made the first important contributions to the knowledge and science of

flight. Otto Lilienthal gathered a great deal of information from the study of birds. He was probably the first to realize the importance of the curved wing surface which is the basis of the modern airplane. Unfortunately he was one of the young pioneers who died in glider experiments.

But it was the Wright brothers, Orville and Wilbur, who made the real breakthrough to a power-driven heavier-than-air craft which they flew on December 17, 1903, at Kitty Hawk, North Carolina. They had first experimented with a two-wing kite in 1899. In 1900 they constructed and flew gliders at Kitty Hawk. Finally, in 1903, they built their first airplane which was named the Flyer. It was a

two-wing or biplane, with a twelve-horsepower gasoline engine. The wings were wood frames covered with cotton cloth. The important advance that the Wright brothers had made was to invent a means of preserving balance in flight. This was done by controlling the tips of the wings with wires which were attached to the pilot's waist as he lay in the center of the lower wing. Now a plane could take off under its own power, and its pilot could have some measure of control in the air. This was the true forerunner of the airplane as we know it today.

Although planes today have undergone many improvements and changes in design from the early Wright plane, they all must still rely on wings and air. There are four basic forces which act on a plane in flight. These are gravity, lift, thrust and drag.

Gravity is the natural force which pulls everything down to the earth. The force on an airplane that acts to overcome the pull of gravity is called lift. Lift is a force which uses the air that surrounds our planet earth. Air exists as an invisible mixture of gases, mostly oxygen and nitrogen. The air which makes it possible for planes to fly is also the air we breathe to stay alive. Most of the force necessary to lift an airplane into the air is produced by the flow of air across the upper surface of the wings.

To understand how lift works as a force, we must first understand some of the properties of air. Through the work of a Swiss mathematician, Daniel Bernoulli, we know that a liquid or a gas, like air, when speeded up, loses pressure.

You can see this principle at work if you hold a long strip of paper up to your mouth and blow across the top surface. You might think that the paper would be forced down by your blowing air, but instead the paper rises as you blow. The faster and harder you blow, the higher the paper rises at the loose end. By speeding up the air, you have made it lose pressure on the top of the paper. The normal pressure on the undersurface of the paper will lift it.

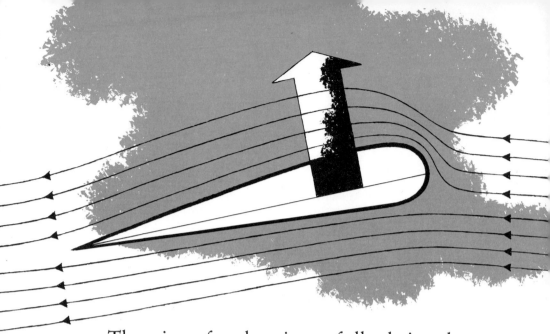

The wing of a plane is carefully designed so that its top surface is a curve and the bottom surface generally is straight. As the wing passes through the air, the air going across the curved top has a longer distance to travel than the air passing under the wing. Since the air on top has farther to go because of the curve, it must travel faster. As a result, the air moving over the top loses pressure while the air moving underneath the wing remains the same. The air under the wing, with its higher pressure, then lifts the wing up. This force upwards is called lift. In order to get the lift force from the speeded-up air, the plane must be propelled forward at a fast speed. This forward motion provided by the engine is called thrust.

Just as lift opposes gravity, thrust opposes drag. Drag is the natural force which slows down the plane as it travels through the air. Drag is created by the friction of the air against the fuselage, or body, and wings of the plane as it moves forward.

For a plane to fly properly, there must be a balancing of these four forces: lift against gravity, thrust against drag.

The wings use the air to create lift and keep the airplane flying. To get added lift the plane's angle of attack must be increased. This is the angle at which the wing cuts through the air. The nose of the plane is pointed up slightly so that the wing is at an upward angle to the plane's line of flight.

Thrust is provided by the airplane engine which supplies the power to move the plane at a fast enough speed for there to be enough lift to make it fly. There are different kinds of engines, but they all do the same job. They move the plane forward fast enough so that it can get lift from its wings.

The earliest airplane engine was a small internal combustion engine which used gasoline as a fuel. Internal combustion means that the fuel is burned inside the engine itself. A car engine is also an internal combustion engine. The power the engine creates is used to turn a propeller.

A propeller is a wooden or metal blade mounted on the engine which spins around very fast as the engine turns. The shape of the propeller blade is important. It is built like a small wing and it acts in the same way. The front of the propeller, that part facing forward on the plane, is curved like the top of the wing surface. As the propeller spins, the air moving across the curved part has a greater distance to travel than the air moving across the rear of the blade. The air in front loses pressure as it moves faster over the longer distance of the curved side of the blade. The propeller is pushed forward as the higher-pressure air behind the propeller moves toward the lower-pressure air in front of the spinning blade. The plane is pulled forward by the propeller as it turns. Many small airplanes use this type of engine and propeller.

The next major improvement in airplane engines was the development of the turboprop jet engine. This engine combines the use of a propeller or prop with a jet engine. A jet engine is a simple engine which uses expanding gases to give the engine power. In all jet engines air is

drawn into the engine from the outside and compressed or squeezed together. A fuel is then injected into this compressed air and ignited. As the fuel and air mixture burn, gases are created which are much greater in volume than the air and fuel. These expanding gases are then pushed out the rear of the jet by their own expanding forces. A jet prop engine uses the same principle as a simple jet engine, but it has a turbine or fan-like device inside, which is turned by the expanding gases as they rush out of the rear of the engine. This turbine turns the propeller while the remaining force of the expanding gases assists in the thrust of the airplane.

A toy balloon is a simple example of how a jet engine works. If you take an ordinary balloon, fill it with air and then release it, it will fly just as a jet flies. The air rushing out of the opening in the balloon forces the balloon through the air. This is an example of one of the basic laws of physics, which states that when there is a force in one direction—in this

case the air escaping from the balloon—there is also an equal but opposite force in the other direction. This is what moves the balloon away from the escaping air.

The next development in airplane engines was the invention of the turbojet engine. The turbojet is the most common engine built for the commercial or military planes of today. The turbojet is like the turboprop but has no propeller, as there is enough force in the expanding gases as they are pushed out the rear of the engine to force the plane forward at a high speed. Turbojet engines have two sets of turbines, one in front of the combustion or burning chamber and another behind. The turbine in front sucks or pulls a large amount of air into the combus-

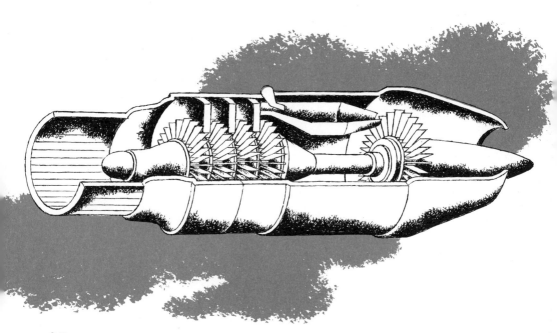

tion chamber where the fuel is added and where the mixture is burned. The expanding gases which are created by the burning fuel and air then rush past the second turbine and turn it. The second turbine supplies the force for the first turbine at the front and is also used to generate electricity for the controls and other supplemental parts of the plane. A turbojet is very efficient at high speeds, but it uses a large amount of fuel and it has caused some pollution problems with its large amount of burned gases and the loud noises it makes when landing and taking off. As the turbojet has become more widely used, airports have had to have longer runways. This is because of the high speeds of the landings and take-offs that these planes require as they have gotten larger and heavier.

When a plane has been designed and built, man as the pilot must set in motion the forces that make it fly. There are many kinds of planes, large and small, but they all use the same basic operations to fly.

Once in the air, the pilot of the plane must have control over where he wants to go. If he wants to turn right and drop a hundred feet, he must have the means to do so. If he wants to climb to a higher altitude, he must have the controls to do this also.

The earlier planes, like the one built by the Wright brothers, were difficult to control in flight. Most of them could only travel in one direction, and there was little if any way to change altitude. Gradually designs were improved so that today pilots have a great deal of control and maneuverability.

The pilot changes the direction of a plane by putting into practice some of the principles you use in steering a bicycle. You have handlebars to guide the bicycle to the right or to the left. This works well when you are riding slowly. But when you are traveling faster, you also have to use your body to change direction. You lean to the right or to the left. This leaning into the turn makes it much easier to turn smoothly at higher speeds. A skilled rider can steer his bicycle without using the handlebars at all, but just by using the weight of his body.

A pilot uses this leaning to change direction when he is flying. He doesn't move his body, but he does lean the plane itself into the direction he wants to turn, using a rudder on the tail and ailerons on the wings.

A rudder is a straight up and down, or vertical, piece on the tail of the plane which can be moved from side to side. It acts much the same as a boat rudder acts to turn a boat in the water. The pilot turns the rudder by means of foot pedals. When the rudder is moved to the right, the air pushing against it pushes the nose of the plane to the right, and when it is moved to the left the plane's nose is pushed to the left.

If the pilot only changed the direction of the rudder, the plane would turn but it would not turn efficiently. To turn properly the pilot must learn to lean the plane into the turn just as the bicycle rider leans into a curve. He does this by lowering one wing and raising the other. The pilot uses the ailerons to raise and lower the plane's wings. Ailerons are short sections at the back or trailing edge of the wings. When the pilot moves the control stick or steering wheel to the left, the aileron on the left wing goes up and the one on the right wing goes down. This leans or rolls the plane to the left.

Ailerons control the lean or roll of the plane by using the force of lift. For example, when the stick is moved to the left, the aileron on the left wing goes up. This reduces the amount of lift on that wing, because it reduces the amount of curve on the wing surface. The left wing will drop as the lift force is reduced. When the right aileron is lowered, the lift force on that wing is increased because the curved surface at the top of that wing has been lengthened and the air flowing over it has an even longer distance to travel. This increases the lift force and the right wing goes up.

When the plane turns, the pilot is also changing the balance between thrust and drag, and he must adjust for this change. The pilot must raise the nose of the plane slightly because the lowering of one wing and the raising of the other will produce more drag and less lift force than when the plane is flying on a level flight path. By raising the nose the pilot can bring the forces of thrust and drag back into balance again. To raise the nose of the plane, however, he must increase his engine power and adjust the plane's elevators which are located on the flat or horizontal part of the tail section. The tail section of an airplane is made up of both a rudder and a pair of elevators, one on either side of the rudder. The elevators are horizontal surfaces which can be moved up or down. The pilot moves the elevators by pushing the control stick forward or back. When he pulls back he moves the elevators up. As the elevators move up, the air flowing across them is deflected or pushed upward, which forces the tail of the plane down. As the

tail drops the nose of the plane goes up. Then the
angle of attack is greater, the lift is greater, and
if the engine power is increased the plane will
climb. If the pilot wants to lower the nose of the
plane, he pushes the control stick forward.

Controlling and guiding the plane while it is
flying is simpler than the taking-off and landing
operations. For taking off, the pilot first makes
a complete check of all his instruments and controls to see that they are working properly. Next

he starts the engine and speeds it up until he has full power. As the plane moves down the runway, the pilot starts with the control stick slightly forward which keeps the plane down on the ground until it has enough speed to take off and also raises the tail section in preparation for the actual takeoff. As the plane speeds up and reaches takeoff velocity, the pilot gently eases the control stick back. This pulls the nose up and the plane takes off. If he pulls back too soon, there will not be enough speed to give sufficient lift to the wings. If he waits too long, he may not have enough space on the runway to complete his takeoff. During the takeoff the rudder and ailerons are in a neutral position and are not used.

Landing a plane is the more difficult of the two maneuvers. The basic idea for landing is to slow the speed of the plane down as much as possible without losing control and to allow it to come in gently at a proper angle to the ground, so that the shock of hitting the ground is as small as possible.

To land a pilot stalls or slows the plane down by using the force of gravity against the force of thrust from the engine. If the plane is put into a slight climbing angle but not given enough

power to climb, it will slow down. This is the preparation for a landing. As the plane slows down, the lift is reduced. To increase drag and thus slow down the plane even more, the nose of the plane is raised. This is a stall. If the pilot is experienced, he will make the plane slow down so much that the actual landing of the plane can hardly be felt. Once on the ground the pilot puts the brakes on and taxies up to the terminal.

On the large commercial airliners there are extensions on the trailing edge of each wing which can be extended or drawn back into the wing. These wing extensions are called flaps.

The purpose of a flap is to increase greatly the curve of the wing surface. When the flap is extended, there is more lift. In normal flight the flaps are retracted into the wing as the extra amount of lift is not needed. When a commercial airliner is landing, the pilot extends the flaps, which increases lift but also increases the drag on the plane and slows it down. To compensate for the increase of drag, the pilot will increase the thrust of the engines so that the proper amount of lift is maintained. Once the plane touches the ground the pilot is able to reverse

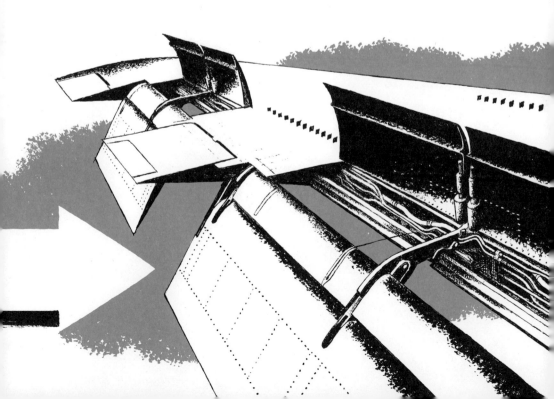

the force of the engines so that their power can be used to slow the plane down. This reversing of the engine thrust often sounds very loud and can be heard by the passengers just as the plane touches the ground.

The part of the plane which touches the ground first is the landing gear. The most common landing gear is two wheels, generally placed one under each wing. Sometimes these are retractable, which means they can be raised once the plane is in the air and tucked either into the body of the plane or into the underpart of the wings, much as a bird tucks its feet up when it is in the air. Retractable landing gear is an advantage because it reduces the drag of the air when the plane is flying. Some of the larger planes have a retractable nose wheel near the front of the plane. Many of the early planes as well as the light planes of today have a skid or a wheel under the tail. Other kinds of landing gear include floats or pontoons for planes that land on water and skis for planes landing on snow.

The early planes did not have all the instruments that are normally found in the modern planes of today. In the early days of flying a pilot would have to follow railroad tracks and highways to find his destination, and he could never fly at night or when it was very foggy or the weather was bad. Now pilots have radar and radio communication which allows them to fly straight to their destination even when it is bad weather and they cannot see. Among the other most common instruments that the pilot relies on are the air speed indicator which tells him

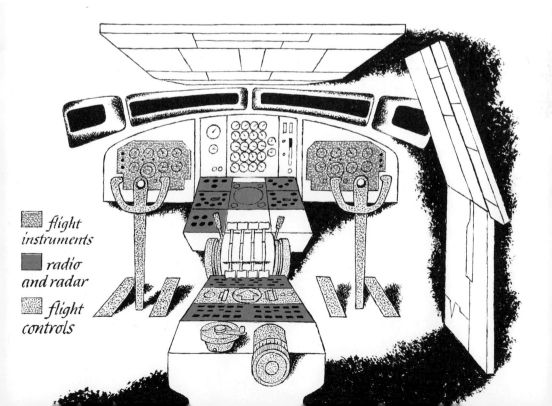

flight instruments

radio and radar

flight controls

how fast he is flying, the compass which tells him direction, and all the gauges and dials which tell him how well his engine is working—fuel, oil pressure and temperature, much like the indicators on your family car.

When a plane flies at very high altitudes, as commercial airliners do, the air is thinner and there is less drag on the plane. Temperatures drop as the altitude increases, the air pressure gets less and breathing becomes more difficult. The lack of pressure can be dangerous for people if they are not protected by a pressurized cabin. The cabin has to be pressurized and heated so that the pilot, crew and passengers are kept as comfortable as if the plane were still on the ground.

All the inventors and scientists who have contributed to the development of the airplane as we know it today have actually made our world seem smaller. We can now travel from continent to continent and see distant lands in a matter of hours. It took the early settlers months to reach

our shores from Europe, and they had to live
through storms and high seas in the most un-
comfortable conditions. Now we think nothing

of flying to Europe in comfort in a matter of six or seven hours. It will take even less time as more planes like the supersonic transport planes are built which fly faster than the speed of sound. But with each larger and faster plane designed and built, the pollution problems they cause must be taken care of too. One of the worst is that of noise. As planes take off and land, the noise that they produce makes it almost impossible to live or work very near airports. The burning gases which escape from the jet engines as the plane flies are also a source of pollution. If man will devote as much time and effort to eliminating the pollution problems as he does to the development of faster and bigger planes, we may see the day when our skies are clear once more and the noise level reduced.

Man has not been able to accomplish flight with the beauty and grace of a bird soaring unaided through the skies. But he has been able to master the art of flying by creating machines to carry him. It may still be the dream of man to fly without the heavy machine, and he is always striving to design new and better kinds of planes. But he will probably have to be content with his natural place on earth, for he will always have to rely on machines to take him up into the air and beyond into outer space.

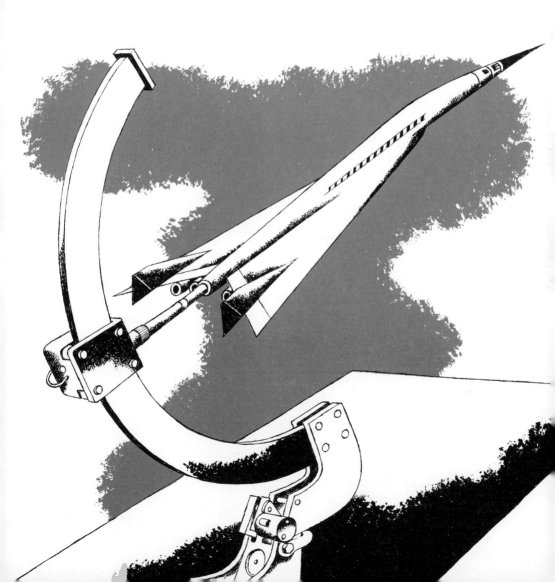

Pick a Powerpuff Path

buttercup's
monster
challenge

by Tracey West

Scholastic Inc.
New York • Toronto • London • Auckland • Sydney
Mexico City • New Delhi • Hong Kong • Buenos Aires

ISBN 0-439-33251-6

Copyright © 2002 by Cartoon Network.

CARTOON NETWORK, the logo, THE POWERPUFF GIRLS, and all related characters and elements are trademarks of and © Cartoon Network.

(s02)

Published by Scholastic Inc. All rights reserved.

SCHOLASTIC and associated logos are trademarks and/or registered trademarks of Scholastic Inc.

Cover and interior illustrations by Christopher Cook

Inked by Bill Alger

Designed by Mark Neston

12 11 10 9 8 7 6 5 4 3 2 1   2 3 4 5 6 7/0

Printed in the U. S. A.

First Scholastic printing, April 2002

Read This First!

Sugar...Spice...and Everything Nice...

These were the ingredients chosen to create the perfect little girl. But Professor Utonium accidentally added an extra ingredient to the concoction—Chemical X!

And thus, The Powerpuff Girls were born! Using their ultra superpowers, Blossom, Bubbles, and Buttercup have dedicated their lives to fighting crime and the forces of evil!

But now, The Powerpuff Girls need your help! In every Pick a Powerpuff Path, you will take on the role of one of the characters and help save the day.

In this adventure, you'll be Buttercup, the super-tough Powerpuff Girl, as she and her sisters race to mysterious Monster Isle, home to all of the monsters that attack Townsville. A monster named Orgon has challenged Buttercup to prove that she is the toughest one around— on Monster Isle as well as in Townsville—and she is not about to back down. Buttercup's adventures will be different depending on the choices you make. After you choose a path, follow along to see where the story takes you.

When you're done, you can start over and make new choices that will take you in a different direction.

Are you all set? Great, because Orgon is waiting for you on Monster Isle—and you don't want to make him impatient!

MONSTER ISLE

BUTTERCUP OF
THE POWERPUFF GIRLS
TOWNSVILLE

SPECIAL DELIVERY!

The city of Townsville! Where on some days, you'll find monsters stomping through the streets—because, as everyone knows, monsters love to fight and make a mess!

Thank goodness for The Powerpuff Girls! Blossom, Bubbles, and Buttercup are the best monster fighters around. Every monster that now invades Townsville is soon sent home to Monster Isle with its tentacles between its legs.

The Girls had never been to Monster Isle. But that changed one morning, when Professor Utonium approached the Girls holding an envelope in one hand.

"Buttercup, this just came for you—special delivery!" the Professor said.

Buttercup looked at the envelope. "It's from Monster Isle," she said, tearing it open.

"What's it say? What's it say?" asked Blossom and Bubbles eagerly.

Buttercup read the letter:

"'Attention, Buttercup! I am Orgon, the toughest monster on Monster Isle. I have defeated every monster on the isle. Now I am looking for an opponent who is worthy of battling me. I hear that you are the toughest member of The Powerpuff Girls. If you accept my challenge, come to Monster Isle today at three o'clock. Sincerely, Orgon.'"

Blossom's eyes narrowed. "Hey, who says *you're* the toughest Powerpuff?" she asked Buttercup. "What about me and Bubbles?"

"You guys are tough, too," Buttercup said. "But, Blossom, you're the leader. Everyone knows that."

"That's true," said Blossom.

Buttercup turned to Bubbles. "And you're the..."

"...The joy and the laughter!" Professor Utonium chimed in quickly.

"See?" Buttercup said. "So I've got to take this Orgon guy up on his challenge."

"This sounds fishy to me," said Blossom. "It might be some kind of trap. We'll go with you."

"Okay," Buttercup said reluctantly. This was something that she really had wanted to do herself, but her sister had a point.

Buttercup started to zip toward the window, but Professor Utonium put his arm out to stop her.

"Wait a minute, Buttercup," he said. "I've been working on an experimental Monster Mix-up spray. If Orgon's challenge turns out to be a trap, the Monster Mix-up spray should help keep you safe. One squirt causes a monster to get all confused, giving you the advantage for a few moments. I can have a batch ready for you in half an hour."

Buttercup glanced at the clock. It was already 2:30. If she waited for the Monster Mix-up, she'd be late for her meeting with Orgon at three o'clock. Then again, the Professor's repellent would be a great thing to have on Monster Isle. Who knows how many monsters she and her sisters would have to fight there?

"What do you want to do, Buttercup?" asked Bubbles.

If Buttercup decides to wait for the Monster Mix-up spray, turn to page 10.

If Buttercup decides to leave right away, turn to page 12.

7

"That's probably just the sound of more lava losers headed this way," said Buttercup. "They don't know who they're up against."

Buttercup and her sisters bravely flew right above the group of angry lava monsters.

"If ice breath works on lava, it must work on lava monsters, too!" Blossom cried. "I think you guys need to chill out!"

Blossom blasted the lava monsters with her ice breath. The monsters froze like statues.

"Don't worry," Bubbles said. "You'll thaw out soon."

"Come on, Girls!" Buttercup said. "I'm supposed to meet Orgon in five minutes!"

The Girls started to fly away—but stopped in their tracks when another group of monsters came trooping up the volcano.

This new group of monsters didn't look like the lava monsters, though. In fact, they looked like they were made of ice.

"Ice monsters!" Bubbles cried.

"Your ice breath won't work on us!" growled their leader.

Buttercup felt her blood begin to boil. "Let's take care of these Popsicles!" she told her sisters.

Zap! Wham! Zoom! Blossom, Bubbles, and Buttercup charged at the ice monsters.

"We'll melt you like ice cream on a hot day!" Buttercup cried, poised to attack again.

"STOP!" someone bellowed.

Continue on page 59.

Buttercup decided to wait for the Monster Mix-up spray. When it was ready, Professor Utonium handed her a spray can. She tucked the can into her belt, then turned to her sisters.

"Let's go, Girls!" Buttercup cried.

The three sisters zipped out the window. Buttercup took the lead as they headed to the waterfront.

"Monster Isle is straight ahead," Buttercup said.

"And so are those storm clouds," Blossom pointed out.

Buttercup looked into the distance. Thick black clouds loomed over the horizon. "Let's fly through the storm," Buttercup said. "A little rain won't hurt us."

"Maybe not," said Blossom. "But what about lightning and winds? I say it's safer if we dive underwater to swim under the storm."

Blossom had a good point. But flying would be faster. Buttercup thought about the best course to take.

If the Girls fly through the storm,
turn to page 58.

If the Girls dive underwater to swim under the storm,
turn to page 22.

The Girls decided to make a quick exit. They swiftly flew off through the trees and soon found themselves in a sunny garden.

"Ooh, look at all the pretty flowers," Bubbles said.

Blossom didn't think the flowers looked pretty. There was something creepy about them. She flew over to one big, bell-shaped flower and peered inside. Rows of sharp teeth snapped at her face!

"These aren't ordinary plants," Blossom warned. "These are monster plants. We'd better get out of here!"

Buttercup agreed. She started to zip forward—until she realized she couldn't move.

She looked down. A thick green vine had wrapped around her legs. Another vine was slowly wrapping around her middle.

"Oh, no!" cried Blossom and Bubbles. The same thing was happening to them.

"I think it's time to weed this garden, Girls!" Buttercup shouted.

If Buttercup blasts the vines with her eye beams, turn to page 25.

If Buttercup hits the vines with a power-punch, turn to page 43.

"There's no time to waste," Buttercup said. "Let's just go without the Monster Mix-up spray!"

Buttercup and her sisters flew away across the water. Soon Buttercup could see a small island in the distance. A tall, cone-shaped mountain rose up in the center of the island, surrounded by trees.

"That must be Monster Isle," Blossom guessed. "But where will we find Orgon?"

"Let's head for the shore," Buttercup suggested. "We can start searching for him there."

The Girls landed on the sandy beach and looked around. There was no sign of monsters anywhere. A leafy green jungle bordered the sand. Bubbles spotted a path at the start of the jungle, and the Girls decided to follow it.

Soon the path forked into two directions—left and right. A sign had been planted where the path forked. Buttercup read the words aloud:

"'Welcome, Buttercup! To find Orgon, go this way.'"

Right underneath the words, someone had painted an arrow pointing left.

But right underneath that, someone had painted an arrow pointing right!

"How do we know which arrow is the real one that leads to Orgon?" Bubbles asked.

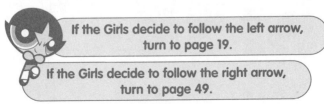

If the Girls decide to follow the left arrow, turn to page 19.

If the Girls decide to follow the right arrow, turn to page 49.

Buttercup decided to take the unmarked left path. It led to a wooded area. The Girls flew for a while, then stopped to rest against a tall tree.

"This path seems to go on forever," Bubbles moaned. "We're never going to find Orgon."

"I can help you find Orgon," said a voice.

The Girls jumped. The *tree* was talking to them! Buttercup could make out a face in its wrinkly bark.

"Another monster plant!" Buttercup cried. "Let's zap it!"

But the tree monster just smiled. "Don't worry, Girls. I don't mean you any harm. I'd be happy to help you."

"Oh, yeah?" Buttercup said, suspicion in her voice.

"Orgon lives at the top of the tallest mountain on the Isle," said the tree monster. "If you fly above the trees, you'll see it."

"Yeah, well, thanks," said Buttercup. "Come on, Girls."

"Wait!" said the tree monster. "Orgon *lives* on the mountain. But he always *trains* for his battles in the jungle. He could be in either place."

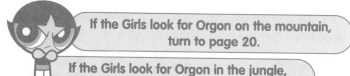

If the Girls look for Orgon on the mountain, turn to page 20.

If the Girls look for Orgon in the jungle, turn to page 39.

Buttercup decided to trust Calvin. After all, he did look pretty scared. He'd be foolish to mess with them now.

"All right," Buttercup said. "Tell me what you know about Orgon, and if I feel like it, I'll let you go. But no tricks!"

"Oh, thank you, thank you," Calvin said. "I'll tell you Orgon's secret. You see, he has a weak spot. He's very ticklish behind his right ear."

"Right ear. Got it," Buttercup said. "But where do we find Orgon?"

"I don't know!" Calvin wailed. "Orgon might be at home—he lives at the top of Monster Isle Mountain. Or, he might be at Monster Isle Stadium— I think I heard him say that he was planning to wait for you there."

"All right," said Buttercup. "I guess you've told us all you know." She let go of Calvin. "Now scram!"

Calvin left a trail of slime behind him as he slithered off into the foliage.

The Girls flew high above the trees, looking for any sign of Orgon. Buttercup could see the two places that Calvin had mentioned: a mountain that rose so high it touched the bottoms of the clouds, and what looked like some kind of sports arena.

"Well, where should we go?" Bubbles asked Buttercup.

If the Girls decide to land on the mountain, turn to page 24.

If the Girls decide to land in the stadium, turn to page 60.

15

Buttercup was too charged up to pay attention to Blossom. First, she went after the blue monster, then she doubled back and attacked the pink monster.

While Buttercup was racing after the pink monster, the can of Monster Mix-up fell out of her belt. The nozzle hit the ground and sprayed a cloud of purple smoke at her sisters.

When the smoke cleared, Buttercup saw a horrible sight. Her sisters had turned into monsters! Blossom and Bubbles were both as tall as trees. Their skin was covered with fur. Blossom had a horn growing out of her head, and Bubbles had a large pair of leathery wings.

"You're monsters!" Buttercup yelled, but her voice sounded deeper and stranger.

"You are, too!" Blossom yelled back. Buttercup looked down and saw that her sister was right.

"The Professor said that his Monster Mix-up spray was experimental," Blossom said. "I bet he didn't know what the effect on *people* would be!"

As Blossom talked, Buttercup saw that the two real monsters had left the scene.

"Hey, this might not be so bad," said Buttercup. "I mean, we look pretty cool."

"Speak for yourself," Blossom said.

"Yeah," said Bubbles. "We won't be able to ride our bicycles anymore. We're too big!"

Suddenly, another shadow fell across the cave. A scaly orange monster faced them. He had a spiky tail and his arms bulged with muscles.

"I am Orgon!" he said in a booming voice.

Continue on page 44.

Buttercup stopped. "What is it, Blossom?"

"Use the Monster Mix-up spray that the Professor gave you," Blossom said.

Why not? Buttercup thought. It might be fun to see if the monsters really became confused. She grabbed the can of Monster Mix-up from her belt and aimed it at the monsters. A cloud of purple smoke poured out as Buttercup emptied the spray can.

"Whoops," Buttercup realized. "All gone!"

But the Monster Mix-up spray had done its job. The two monsters had stopped in their tracks. One was scratching its head. The other was walking in circles. They seemed to have forgotten all about the battle.

Bubbles cheered, "You did it!"

"Thanks to the Professor," Buttercup said. "Now let's get down to business. I've got to find Orgon."

Buttercup stepped out of the cave. There was a mountain just up ahead.

"Let's head over there and see if Orgon's around," Buttercup suggested.

Continue on page 50.

18

"Let's take the left path," Buttercup said. "There's a fifty-fifty chance it's the correct one."

The three sisters flew down the left path. Giant green leaves tickled their faces as they flew past.

Suddenly, Buttercup, who was in the lead, stopped abruptly. "Uh-oh," she said. "Check this out."

Blossom and Bubbles caught up to Buttercup and saw that a huge gray boulder blocked the path in front of them. The sides of the boulder disappeared into the jungle on either side. It rose up above the trees and into the clouds.

"Should we go back?" Bubbles wondered out loud.

"It can't be *that* high," Blossom said. "Let's see if we can fly over it."

"Why bother?" Buttercup said. "Let's just use our lasers to blast a hole in it. We can fly right through."

If the Girls try to fly over the boulder, turn to page 30.

If the Girls try to blast a hole in the boulder, turn to page 26.

19

Buttercup led the Girls to the tall mountain.

"Orgon is supposed to be the biggest, baddest monster on Monster Isle," she explained. "So it makes sense that his hideout is in the biggest, tallest place on the island."

The Girls flew closer and closer. About halfway up the mountain, Buttercup spotted two figures standing on a plateau.

"Monsters!" Buttercup called to her sisters. "Let's see if one of them is Orgon."

The Girls swooped down. As they got closer, Buttercup could see that one monster was blue and the other was pink. They each had sharp claws and bulging eyes.

Suddenly, the two monsters saw The Powerpuff Girls flying toward them. They began to stomp their feet and wave their hands. The ground beneath them shook.

"Are they friendly?" Bubbles wondered.

"I think they're getting ready to attack," Blossom said. "What do you want to do, Buttercup?"

If Buttercup thinks they should battle the monsters, turn to page 62.

If Buttercup thinks they should talk to the monsters first, turn to page 37.

Buttercup decided the Girls should go underwater to avoid the wind in the storm clouds. The Girls dove into the ocean and tried to stay on course by keeping straight ahead. But it was difficult to see in the dark water. Buttercup swam ahead of her sisters and used her green eye beams to light the way.

Suddenly, the Girls found themselves in a dry place. Buttercup used her eye beams to examine the area around them. They seemed to be in some kind of a cave.

"We must have swum in through a hole," Blossom said.

Suddenly, Buttercup saw two red lights in the darkness. "Look over there!" she said, pointing. "Those lights must be attached to a boat or something. That must be the way out of the cave."

The Girls swam toward the lights. As they got closer, Buttercup realized that the lights weren't attached to any boat.

They were the eyes of a sea monster! Its big head rested on two scaly feet.

"Hello, Buttercup," said the sea monster in a smooth voice. "My name is Draconia."

"How did you know my name?" Buttercup asked, startled.

The sea monster smiled. "All monsters know who you are. But I know a lot of other things, too," she said. "For instance, I know where you're going. And I know how to help you. But first, you must answer my riddle."

Buttercup thought about what to do. Maybe the sea monster was telling the truth, and she really *did* want to help Buttercup in her challenge with Orgon. But Buttercup was running out of time before her meeting with Orgon—what if playing the sea monster's game made her late for the challenge?

If Buttercup decides to answer the riddle, turn to page 33.

If Buttercup refuses to play the sea monster's game, turn to page 38.

"Let's try the mountain," Buttercup finally decided.

"Uh, Buttercup," Blossom said, "I don't think this is a mountain. It's a volcano!"

Blossom was floating over a gaping hole, over-flowing with bubbling lava!

"Blossom, use your ice breath to stop the volcano from erupting!" said Buttercup. "The lava could overrun the whole island!"

"What if there are lava monsters living in the volcano?" worried Bubbles. "Blossom's ice breath might hurt them."

Streams of icy wind poured from Blossom's mouth. The ice formed a thick cap over the volcano, cooling the lava.

"Nice work, Blossom," Buttercup said.

"How dare you!" an angry voice cried.

A group of monsters had appeared. Their red-hot, rocky bodies smoked.

"There *are* lava monsters living in this volcano," said the lead monster. "And we are they. You've ruined our home!"

"Looks like we're in for a fight," Blossom said, preparing to attack. "I'm sorry I didn't listen to you, Bubbles."

"Wait!" yelled Bubbles. "Someone is calling for help down the mountain!"

If the Girls get ready to fight the lava monsters, turn to page 8.

If the Girls decide they should respond to the cry for help, turn to page 34.

24

Buttercup zapped the vines with a green eye beam blast.

The vines wriggled as the eye beams made contact. Then they turned brown and began to shrink. Buttercup easily slipped out of the withered vines. Blossom and Bubbles used their eye beams to free themselves, too.

"That was a di-*vine* solution," Blossom joked, although she was clearly still a little shaken by the experience.

"Let's get out of here fast," Bubbles said.

The Girls quickly flew to the garden's border, where they found two paths leading out. One path went to the left, and wasn't marked at all. The other path led to the right. It was marked by a wood sign that read MONSTER STADIUM, THIS WAY. "I wonder if that's where monsters have battles," Buttercup said. "Maybe Orgon is there."

"Maybe," Blossom said. "Or maybe it's some kind of trick."

"Which way should we go?" Bubbles asked.

If the Girls choose the path to Monster Stadium, turn to page 35.

If the Girls choose the unmarked path, turn to page 14.

25

"Let's just blast a hole," Buttercup said. "Then the path will be opened up for everyone."

Buttercup aimed a green eye beam at the giant rock. The boulder began to move, and an angry scream filled the air. Buttercup realized with astonishment that the boulder was alive.

The giant rock was really a giant rock monster!

The angry monster towered over the Girls. Buttercup couldn't even see its head, it was so high in the sky.

The monster bellowed angrily. A giant arm made of rock swooped down upon them. The Girls flew out of the way just in time.

"Hey, cut that out!" Buttercup cried. She responded with a super-kick to the monster's shin. But the monster didn't even seem to notice it.

"How are we supposed to fight this guy?" Buttercup wondered.

"Maybe we can confuse it," said Blossom. "Follow me!"

Buttercup and Bubbles followed Blossom up to the monster's head.

Blossom flew in circles around its face. "Try and catch me, Rocky!" she called to the monster.

Buttercup and Bubbles followed Blossom's lead. They all flew in circles around the monster's head. Soon the monster began to sway back and forth, like it was dizzy.

"Look out below!" Buttercup yelled.

The rock monster grabbed its head with its giant hands. It moaned, then crashed to the ground below.

Monster Isle shook for a few seconds, then all was quiet again.

"We defeated the Rock Monster!" cheered Blossom.

"Now let's go find Orgon," said Buttercup. "There's a jungle up ahead. I bet that's where he is."

"Wait!" Bubbles said. "I think I hear someone crying by that mountain over there. Maybe somebody needs our help."

Buttercup frowned. "I think you're as dizzy as the rock monster, Bubbles," she said. "I don't hear anything."

"So, where are we going?" asked Blossom. "To the jungle, or to the mountain?"

If the Girls decide to follow the sound Bubbles heard and head for the mountain, turn to page 34.

If the Girls keep going toward the jungle, turn to page 39.

27

"You're right," Blossom said. "We shouldn't let Calvin get away with trying to trap us."

As quick as a flash, The Powerpuff Girls flew out of the cage and circled Calvin. Buttercup glared at the sluglike monster. "You think you're the toughest monster in this place, Calvin? We'll see about that."

"I don't want to fight you!" Calvin protested. "The other monsters think I'm a loser. I just wanted to show them that I could do something big and important by capturing you. I wasn't going to hurt you!"

Buttercup grabbed Calvin by the slimy skin on his neck.

"Now I'm late for my meeting with Orgon, so you're coming with us to see him," she said. "Orgon probably thinks I've chickened out of his challenge. I want him to know what really happened."

"Orgon? No, please don't do that," Calvin said, shivering. "He really is much tougher than me, and he'll be so mad!" Then he got a gleam in his eye. "I'll tell you what," he said. "I know a secret that will help you defeat Orgon. If you let me go, I'll tell you."

"Be careful, Buttercup," said Blossom. "It could be a trick. How do we know that Calvin will tell us the truth?"

If Buttercup decides to listen to what Calvin has to say, turn to page 15.

If Buttercup decides to take Calvin to Orgon, turn to page 36.

28

"I guess it's time to give this stuff a try," Buttercup said, whipping out the can of Monster Mix-up.

Before Orgon could react, Buttercup aimed the spray can at him and pressed on the nozzle. A cloud of purple smoke poured out. Orgon wailed and tried to blow the smoke away.

Buttercup expected Orgon to run away or something. But something went wrong with the Monster Mix-up spray. Orgon seemed to be growing larger and larger!

The monsters in the crowd stomped and cheered as Orgon grew taller and taller. Soon he towered over the stadium.

Buttercup gulped. Fighting a regular monster was one thing. But Orgon was now huge! How was she supposed to beat him?

Buttercup glanced at the can of Monster Mix-up. It had worked on Orgon. Maybe it would work on her, too.

If Buttercup decides to use the Monster Mix-up on herself, turn to page 48.

If Buttercup decides to give the fight her best shot without using the Monster Mix-up, turn to page 53.

Blossom convinced Buttercup that they should fly over the boulder. They flew up, up, up, until finally they saw blue sky peeking over the top of the boulder.

"We made it!" Buttercup said. "Full speed a—heyyyyyyy!"

A giant bird had swooped down from the sky. In a split second, it scooped them all up in its large yellow claws.

"I can't get loose!" Blossom cried. The Girls struggled under the bird's grip but couldn't get free.

The bird flew to the tall mountain in the center of the island. It dropped the Girls inside a huge nest at the very top of the mountain's peak, then perched on the edge.

"*Caaaw! Caaw!*" cried the monster bird.

"It doesn't speak English like some of the monsters around here," Blossom noticed.

"That's okay, I know what she's saying," Bubbles said. Bubbles understood the language of animals—even monster birds. "She thinks we're her children."

Buttercup jumped up. "Well, tell her that she's wrong! We've got things to do."

The bird lowered her beak into the nest. Soon she had a big beetle with wriggling legs hooked onto her beak.

"I think this is our lunch," Bubbles said.

"Gross!" Buttercup said. "We've got to get out of here!"

"Let's fly away really fast," Bubbles said. "She won't be able to catch us."

"There's a jungle right below us," Blossom said. "If we go down there, she'll never find us in all those trees."

Buttercup thought about what to do. They could fly away and hope the bird wouldn't catch them. Hiding out in the jungle wasn't a bad idea—but who knew what waited for them in there? The jungle might be more dangerous than the bird.

If the Girls try to fly away really fast, turn to page 52.

If the Girls try to make it into the jungle, turn to page 39.

31

"I guess I've got nothing to lose," Buttercup said. "What's the riddle?"

The sea monster nodded. "Very good. Here is the riddle. How does the ocean say hello?"

Buttercup was stumped.

"You can do it, Buttercup," Blossom urged.

Buttercup sighed. What kind of a riddle was that? Oceans didn't talk. They were just big bodies of water filled with fish and waves and.... That was it! Buttercup got it.

"It waves!" Buttercup said.

Draconia nodded. "You are correct. And now I will keep my end of the bargain. I know you are going to battle Orgon. He is a tough monster, it's true. But he has one weak spot. He is ticklish behind his left ear."

Buttercup thought about this. "That could come in handy," she said. "Thanks, Draconia!"

"My pleasure," she said. "If you like, you can use my cave to take a shortcut to Monster Isle."

Draconia pointed to a hole in the cave wall. "That tunnel will take you to another cave in the center of Monster Isle."

"Great!" Buttercup said, and the Girls zipped through the tunnel.

Continue on page 41.

33

"If Bubbles is right and somebody needs us, I'd feel terrible if we let them down," Buttercup finally said.

The Girls flew around the mountain, following Bubbles's lead. Soon they discovered Bubbles was right. A yellow baby monster sat on the ground crying. It had a long trunk for a nose. It seemed to be all alone.

"Oh, how cute!" Bubbles cooed, picking it up and cuddling it. "We have to help it find its mommy."

"Uh, I think its mommy found *us*!" Blossom said.

Buttercup looked up. A bigger version of the baby monster was standing on the trail in front of them. A *much* bigger version.

Bubbles gently set the baby down at the mommy monster's feet. The monster made an angry noise and started swinging her trunk back and forth.

"I think we should go before the mommy monster gets madder," Bubbles said. "Everything seems to be okay with the baby, and you've got to find Orgon. We can fly right past the mommy monster."

Blossom pointed just off of the trail. "It looks like there's a garden or something over there," she said. "If we went there, we wouldn't even have to go near the mommy monster."

Whose advice should Buttercup follow?

If Buttercup decides that she and her sisters should fly past the mommy monster, turn to page 42.

If Buttercup decides that she and her sisters should go into the garden, turn to page 11.

34

The Girls flew to Monster Stadium. It was a gigantic sports arena. Monsters of all kinds filled the stands. They held signs that read MONSTERS RULE! and GO, ORGON!

Standing in the middle of the field was a tall orange monster. Sharp spikes dotted his long, strong tail. Muscles bulged from his bulky arms.

"That must be Orgon," Buttercup guessed. The Girls flew down to the field and faced the monster.

"Welcome, Buttercup!" Orgon bellowed. "I see you have accepted my challenge. I have been searching for a worthy opponent on Monster Isle, but no one has been able to defeat me. You are the toughest Powerpuff Girl. Do you think you can beat me?"

Buttercup looked Orgon squarely in the eyes. "Yes, I do!" she replied confidently.

Continue on page 46.

35

Buttercup used her super-strength to hoist Calvin over her head. "You're coming with us, Calvin!"

The Girls flew back down the trail until they came to the sign that had first greeted them. This time, they followed the arrow pointing left to a clearing in the jungle. A big orange monster with a spiky tail stood in the center of the clearing.

"I am Orgon," said the monster. "I see you have accepted my challenge, Buttercup. I thought you had chickened out."

"It wasn't my fault," Buttercup said. She dumped Calvin at Orgon's feet. "This little creep set a trap for me. He was trying to get all the credit for defeating me."

"Calvin has been bugging me since we were in kindergarten," Orgon said angrily. "He's been hiding since I announced that I had challenged you to a battle. I knew he was planning something."

"Well, he's not hiding now," Buttercup said. "Now how about that battle?"

Orgon shook his head. "I invited you here because I was looking for a worthy opponent," Orgon said. "But by stopping Calvin's plans to make himself look tougher than me, you have proven that you are my friend. It would be against the monster code to battle you now."

Buttercup smiled. "I like your style, Orgon," she said.

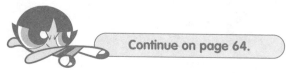

Continue on page 64.

Buttercup shouted down to the monsters. "Hey, is one of you guys Orgon?"

"No!" answered the pink monster. "My name is Orville, and this is my sister, Olive. Orgon is our older brother. That's why we were trying to get your attention."

"That's right," said Olive, the blue monster. "We wanted to talk to you before you go to battle Orgon. He's such a mean bully! He's beaten up every single monster on Monster Isle. And he's always picking on us."

Bubbles frowned. "That's not very nice."

"It certainly isn't," agreed Orville. "That's why we hope Buttercup can teach Orgon a lesson. We know something that can help you."

Buttercup flew up to Orville's face. "Help me? How?" she asked.

"Orgon is ticklish behind his left ear," Orville said. "If you get him in his weak spot, he'll be putty in your hands."

Buttercup liked the sound of that. "Thanks, Orville and Olive," Buttercup said. "So where can we find Orgon, anyway?"

"He's around here somewhere, getting ready," Olive said. "Try checking the other side of the mountain."

"Great!" Buttercup replied, and the Girls zoomed away.

Continue on page 50.

"Sorry, I don't play games with monsters," Buttercup snapped.

That made Draconia angry. She blew three large bubbles from her mouth. A glistening bubble surrounded each Girl and carried them out of the cave, high into the air. The bubbles broke with a *pop!*— sending the Girls falling into a gigantic stadium full of monsters.

Dazed, Buttercup got to her feet. Standing in front of her was a big orange monster with a spiky tail.

"Welcome to Monster Stadium," said the monster, displaying a mouth full of pointed teeth. "I am Orgon, and I challenge you, Buttercup."

"Fine," Buttercup said. "Let's do—"

Orgon opened his mouth and shot a blaze of hot flame at Buttercup. She jumped up just in time.

"No fair!" Buttercup cried. That was a cheap shot. The battle hadn't even started.

"Buttercup, use the Monster Mix-up spray!" Blossom urged.

Buttercup was angry now. Maybe she should use the Monster Mix-up on Orgon. On the other hand, she was here to prove that she was tough. She didn't need a spray to do that.

If Buttercup decides it's time to use the Monster Mix-up, turn to page 29.

If Buttercup wants to battle Orgon on her own terms, turn to page 55.

38

"Let's go to the jungle," Buttercup decided.

The Girls flew ahead to the jungle. Green leaves brushed against their faces as they flew. But they didn't get very far.

An orange monster jumped out on the path in front of them. He had a face like a dragon's and a long, spiked tail. Fierce-looking teeth filled his mouth.

"Welcome, Buttercup!" said the monster in a deep voice. "I am Orgon. No monster on Monster Isle has been able to defeat me in battle yet. That is why I asked you here. As the toughest Powerpuff Girl, you are the only opponent worthy of challenging me. Are you ready?"

"You bet!" Buttercup cried.

"Then let the battle begin!" Orgon roared.

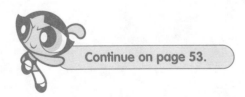

Continue on page 53.

39

The Girls flew through the tunnel. Sure enough, they soon found themselves flying upward. The tunnel opened up into a large cave. Sunlight shone in through the entrance.

"It worked! We're not underwater anymore," Blossom said.

The Girls started to fly toward the mouth of the cave when suddenly a dark shadow fell across them.

Two tall monsters stood at the cave entrance. They looked sort of like dragons, but one was blue and the other was pink.

"Going somewhere, Powerpuff Girls?" asked the blue monster.

"How do you know who we are?" Bubbles asked.

"Are you kidding? Every monster knows who you are. You are legendary on Monster Isle," the blue monster replied.

"Enough talking," shrieked the pink monster. "Let's get them!"

"So you're looking for action, are you?" Buttercup replied. "Well, that's fine with me." She started to zoom in for the attack.

"Wait!" Blossom yelled.

If Buttercup doesn't wait, but immediately blasts the monsters, turn to page 16.

If Buttercup stops and listens to Blossom, turn to page 18.

41

"Let's just fly past her," Buttercup said. "What can she do to us?"

Blossom and Bubbles exchanged looks, but they followed Buttercup as she flew above the mommy monster, who was glaring at them angrily. The baby monster had stopped crying and was now giggling happily as it hugged its mother's leg.

Suddenly, the mommy monster pointed her trunk at them. A spray of slimy green liquid spewed out.

"Gross!" Buttercup cried.

The Girls managed to zip past the mommy monster, avoiding most of the green slime. The baby monster gurgled, letting go of its mother's leg to wave bye-bye as the Girls flew past.

"That was close," Buttercup mumbled.

"Where are we going now?" Blossom asked.

"If we fly higher," suggested Bubbles, "we can get another look at the whole island. Maybe we missed something the first time."

Continue on page 52.

Buttercup smacked the vines with her strongest power-punch, but she couldn't get loose.

Then a tall orange monster stepped through the jungle plants. He looked sort of like a dragon.

"Welcome, Buttercup," said the monster, beating his spiky tail against the ground. "I am Orgon. And thanks to my jungle friends, I have defeated the toughest Powerpuff Girl. Now the other monsters will do whatever I say!"

"You're not tough!" Buttercup shot back. "You didn't beat me yourself. You used a bunch of stupid vines."

Buttercup felt a surge of anger shoot through her. She burst through the vines, easily breaking them this time.

Buttercup pulled the vines off of her sisters. She flew around and around Orgon with the vines until he was tied tightly.

"Who's toughest now?" Buttercup asked.

Orgon hung his head. "You are," he said in a small, defeated voice.

"And don't you forget it!" Buttercup said.

Continue on page 64.

"And I am Buttercup!" Buttercup said. "I got your challenge and I'm here to accept it."

"Buttercup? But you look like a monster," Orgon said.

"It's a long story," Buttercup snapped. Being in monster form was giving her a monster temper. "Are we going to battle, or what?"

"Yes," Orgon replied. "None of the monsters on Monster Isle can defeat me. I'm looking for a real challenge."

Buttercup and Orgon stepped outside the cave and started to battle in a field. Buttercup stomped toward Orgon. The ground shook under her big, furry feet. Orgon stomped closer and closer. The two locked arms.

Buttercup tried to push back Orgon, but he was very strong. She'd have to try something else.

Buttercup wrapped her brand-new tail around Orgon's tail until the two were tied in knots. Lifting off from the ground, she found to her relief that she could still fly.

Orgon dangled from Buttercup's tail. "Help! I'm afraid of heights!" he wailed.

"So you're not so tough after all, are you?" Buttercup chided him.

On the ground below, she could hear Bubbles's voice.

"Buttercup, something's happening! I feel all tingly!" Bubbles shouted.

"I think the Monster Mix-up is wearing off!" added Blossom.

Buttercup was feeling a little funny herself.

"Uh-oh," she told Orgon. "I'd better get you down—whoa!"

Buttercup suddenly transformed back into her old self. Her fur was gone—and so was her tail. Orgon went spiraling to the ground below.

"Hellllp!" yelled Orgon.

"No sweat," responded Buttercup. "I may not be a monster, but I'm still a Powerpuff Girl."

Buttercup zoomed underneath Orgon and caught him before he touched the ground.

"Thanks, Buttercup," Orgon said. "I guess you *are* the toughest after all—*and* the nicest."

Continue on page 64.

Three monsters stepped out onto the sidelines.

"These are the official judges," Orgon explained. "They will decide who is the winner."

"Fine with me," Buttercup said. She shot up into the air, ready to make her first move.

"I'm so tough I can hammer nails with my teeth!" Orgon shouted at her.

"Whatever," Buttercup said. "Now let's start the battle."

"This *is* the battle," Orgon said. "A battle of words."

Buttercup was confused. "What do you mean?" she asked.

"This is how monsters fight on Monster Isle," he said. "We talk tough about ourselves and insult our opponents. If we fought with our bodies, we'd ruin Monster Isle. That would be terrible."

"But I guess you have no problem stomping around—and ruining—Townsville," Blossom muttered.

Buttercup put her arms on her hips. "So this is a fight with words, huh? No problem."

Orgon laughed. "It will not be easy. I am so tough I eat rocks for breakfast."

"Oh yeah?" Buttercup replied. "Is that after your mommy gives you a bubble bath?"

Orgon looked angry. "You still sleep with your teddy bear!" he shouted.

"And you still sleep with the light on!" Buttercup shot back.

"I am so tough that I don't need to sleep!" Orgon thundered.

Buttercup decided to end this fight quickly. If she hurried, she could still make it home in time to watch her favorite cartoons.

"That's it!" Buttercup screamed. "I AM the toughest. I can make mincemeat out of any monster in minutes. I can take whatever you dish out and feed it back to you for dessert. And YOU are nothing but a thumb-sucking, teddy-bear-snuggling, afraid-of-the-dark WIMP!"

"Go, Buttercup!" cheered her sisters.

Orgon began to stammer. "Oh yeah? Well, you're a...I'm a...."

One of the judges banged a gong. "The battle is over. Buttercup is the winner. She is the toughest!"

"I knew that already," Buttercup said. "Now all of *you* know it, too. So remember *that* the next time you decide to come to Townsville—'cause you'll have to deal with me!"

Continue on page 64.

Buttercup decided to spray herself with the Monster Mix-up stuff. As it took effect, she grew taller and taller. Soon she towered above the stadium and faced Orgon.

"Now we're even!" Buttercup said. "Let's battle!"

Orgon and Buttercup stomped their feet, and the whole stadium shook. Monsters shouted as popcorn and sodas flew out of their hands.

Buttercup heard a tiny voice in her ear. "This has got to stop. You two are going to cause an earthquake."

It was Blossom. She took a small spray can from her belt and sprayed both Buttercup and Orgon with it. Soon they were both back to their normal sizes.

"The Professor gave me a can of antidote in case something went wrong," Blossom said. "I'm glad it worked."

"Do you still want to battle?" Buttercup asked.

Orgon shook his head. "No way. I may be tough, but our battle almost destroyed Monster Isle. I would never do anything to hurt my home!"

"Well, that's how *we* feel when you and your pals invade Townsville and start messing things up!" countered Buttercup. "Remember *that* the next time you decide to visit *our* home!"

Continue on page 64.

"Let's take the path to the right," Buttercup suggested. "There's a fifty-fifty chance that this way is correct."

The Girls flew deep into the green, leafy jungle.

Suddenly, a metal cage dropped on top of them! A yellow sluglike monster slid in front of the cage. Six arms wiggled from the monster's sides.

"Are you Orgon?" Buttercup asked the monster angrily.

The monster chuckled. "Oh, no. I am Calvin, the toughest monster on Monster Isle!"

"I thought Orgon was the toughest monster," Blossom said.

Calvin scowled. "That's what *he* thinks. But *I* am the toughest monster, and I'm going to prove it. When the other monsters see that I have trapped The Powerpuff Girls, they will make *me* their king! I will show them that I, Calvin, am the greatest. I, Calvin, am the best monster...."

Calvin was so involved in what he was saying, he was no longer paying attention to the Girls. Blossom quickly bent open the cage bars. "Let's fly away," she whispered. "Calvin's so busy congratulating himself, he probably won't even notice. Then we can go back to helping you find Orgon."

"No way," Buttercup said. "I want to stay and teach Calvin a lesson."

If the Girls sneak out of the cage while Calvin isn't paying attention to them, turn to page 11.

If the Girls decide to confront Calvin, turn to page 28.

49

The Girls flew around the mountain. Soon they spotted a tall orange monster. Bumpy scales covered his skin. Pointy spikes rose from his tail. Muscles bulged on his strong arms.

"I am Orgon!" the monster yelled. "Welcome, Buttercup."

Buttercup landed next to him. "All right, Orgon. I'm here. Now what do you want?" she demanded.

Orgon stomped his feet. "You know what I want," he bellowed. "I want to battle you! Let's see who is tougher. Once I defeat you, I will know I am the strongest creature in the world. All of the other monsters will do my bidding."

"You're on!" Buttercup shot back.

Orgon and Buttercup began to fight. It was a tough battle. Buttercup tried every technique she knew.

That's when Buttercup remembered—Orgon's tickle spot! It might be just what she needed to win.

While Buttercup planned her strategy, Orgon lashed out with his heavy tail. The blow sent her shooting up in the air.

But it was just where Buttercup needed to be. She zoomed down, aiming for Orgon's left ear.

"Tickle, tickle," Buttercup said, tickling the monster behind his left ear.

Orgon began to giggle. "No! Not my tickle spot!"

Buttercup didn't let up. "What's the matter, Orgon? Can't you take it?"

Orgon rolled around on the ground. "Quit it! You win. You're the toughest. Now stop!"

Buttercup stopped and Orgon stood up.

"That was a good match," she told Orgon.

Continue on page 64.

"Good idea, Bubbles," said Buttercup. "Let's fly."

So Buttercup and her sisters soared higher and higher into the sky. Once again, all of Monster Isle was spread out below them. Soon Blossom spotted something. "I think I see two big monsters down there, near that pile of boulders!" she called out.

Sure enough, a couple of big monsters were sleeping in the sun, basking against some large rocks. One was blue, and the other was pink. They both had bumpy scales covering their bodies, and long, spiked tails.

"Maybe one of them is Orgon," Bubbles suggested.

"I don't think Orgon would be sleeping when he's expecting me," Buttercup said. "Besides, they don't look that tough."

"We could wake them up and see if they know where Orgon is," Blossom said.

Buttercup thought about what to do. Waking up the monsters could help them find Orgon. Or it might delay them even further. Buttercup was anxious to find Orgon as soon as possible.

If the Girls decide to wake up the monsters and ask where to find Orgon, turn to page 56.

If the Girls decide to leave the sleeping monsters alone, turn to page 54.

Orgon looked pretty tough, but Buttercup was a Powerpuff Girl, and she never backed down from a fight. She got ready to attack.

But before Buttercup could make a move, another monster stepped in front of her! This monster looked like Orgon, but she wore a white apron around her waist.

"Orgon, what are you doing?" the white-aproned monster snapped.

Orgon lowered his eyes and shuffled his big feet. "Nothing, Mommy."

Orgon's mother shook her head. "You know you are not supposed to battle today!"

"Why not?" asked Buttercup. "I thought all monsters liked to battle."

"Of course," said Orgon's mother. "But Orgon is always so busy battling that he never has time to do his chores. Your room is a mess, young monster!"

"Sorry, Mommy," said Orgon.

Orgon's mother grabbed him by the ear. "You are coming home right now! No battles for you until your room is spotless."

Buttercup stared, her mouth hanging open, as Orgon and his mother left.

"I guess Orgon *isn't* the toughest monster on Monster Isle after all," Blossom said. "His mother is!"

Continue on page 64.

"Let's just try to sneak past them," whispered Buttercup. "I'm almost late for my challenge!"

The Girls quietly flew past the sleeping pink and blue monsters...and found themselves face-to-face with an angry *orange* monster!

"I am Orgon," said the monster, displaying a mouth full of pointy teeth. "Which one of you is Buttercup?"

"I am," Buttercup answered.

Orgon smiled. "Great! Then let the arm wrestling begin!"

Buttercup was confused. "Arm wrestling?"

Orgon explained that on Monster Isle, monsters always arm wrestled to see which one was tougher.

The idea that monsters proved their toughness through arm wrestling seemed silly to Buttercup. But at least this challenge would be easier than an all-out battle.

Orgon and Buttercup faced off, resting their wrestling arms on a rock. It was a close match, but finally, Buttercup felt Orgon's arm give, and she slammed it down onto the rock!

"You win," Orgon said. "Looks like you're the toughest, Buttercup. According to the monster code, you have proved yourself worthy. You're welcome here anytime."

"Thanks, Orgon," Buttercup said.

Continue on page 64.

Buttercup tossed the can of Monster Mix-up spray to her sisters.

"Hold this," she said. "I can take care of this bully on my own."

And Buttercup did just that. She grabbed Orgon by his long tail and started swinging him around and around.

"Hey!" wailed Orgon. "Orville, Olive, come help me!"

"Huh?" Buttercup wondered. A pink monster and a blue monster came out of the stands.

"We'll help you, Brother!" the monsters cried.

Buttercup wasn't worried. "I can take on all three of you," she said.

Then a flash of blue and pink light whizzed past her. Bubbles and Blossom landed beside Buttercup.

"Three against one is no fair," said Blossom. "We'll take care of these two. You worry about Orgon."

While her sisters attacked the other two monsters, Buttercup battled Orgon. It turned out that he wasn't very tough after all.

"Stop!" Orgon wailed. "You're the toughest! I give up!"

"Don't forget us," Blossom said to Buttercup.

"Yeah, we're tough, too," said Bubbles.

Buttercup had to admit they were right. "Thanks for helping me," she said. "I couldn't have done it without you."

Continue on page 64.

"Let's wake them up," Buttercup said. "I don't want to spend all day looking for Orgon without a clue."

Buttercup flew to the pink monster and shook its shoulders. "Hey, monster! Do you know where Orgon is?"

The monster's eyes fluttered open. It looked distressed when it saw Buttercup.

"Oh, no! We fell asleep!" said the pink monster. It nudged the other monster. "Olive, wake up! We fell asleep."

"Oh, no!" said Olive.

"What's wrong?" Bubbles asked.

"I'm Orville, and this is Olive," explained the pink monster. "Orgon is our brother. He's waiting for you at Monster Stadium. He asked us to keep an eye out for you so you'd know where to find him."

"Monster Stadium?" Buttercup asked.

Olive nodded. "It's where the monsters on Monster Isle go to challenge one another. The popcorn there is great!"

Orville and Olive gave the Girls directions to the stadium.

"Thanks!" Buttercup said as she and her sisters flew away.

Continue on page 35.

57

"Let's take a chance and fly through the storm," Buttercup said. "It'll be faster that way."

Blossom and Bubbles followed Buttercup into the thick storm clouds.

Suddenly, Buttercup felt the Monster Mix-up spray can jerk out of her belt and fall into the ocean below.

A strong wind kicked up. The three Girls couldn't fight against it as it blew them onto a sandy beach.

"We're on Monster Isle," Blossom said. "The storm carried us here."

The Girls flew around the island. At the edge of the beach was a moist-looking jungle. Buttercup noticed a sign where the beach ended and the jungle began. She read the words aloud.

"'Welcome, Buttercup! To find Orgon, go this way.'"

Right underneath the words, someone had painted an arrow pointing left.

And right under that, someone else had painted an arrow pointing right!

"How do we know which arrow is the *real* one to Orgon?" Bubbles asked.

If the Girls decide to follow the left arrow, turn to page 19.

If the Girls decide to follow the right arrow, turn to page 49.

Buttercup turned around. A big orange monster had appeared behind them. Sharp spikes dotted his long tail. Muscles bulged from his strong arms.

"I am Orgon," bellowed the monster. "Be gone, ice monsters! Buttercup is here to battle me, not you."

The ice monsters scrambled down the volcano.

"So you're Orgon," said Buttercup. "You really want to battle me?"

Orgon nodded. "Battling the other monsters on this island has become boring. I want a real challenge. Do you accept?"

"Sure," said Buttercup. "Come on!"

Buttercup and Orgon battled with all their might. Finally, Buttercup whizzed behind Orgon and picked him up by the end of his spiky tail. She swung Orgon around and around in circles above her head. Then she let go. Orgon flew high in the air, soared over the volcano's frozen crater, and landed on the other side.

The volcano rumbled as Orgon touched down. Buttercup quickly flew to the monster.

"What do you say now, Orgon?" Buttercup asked. "Am I the toughest?"

Orgon sighed. "You have defeated me, Buttercup," he said. "You are the only worthy opponent I have encountered. Yes, you are the toughest!"

Continue on page 64.

"Let's try the stadium," Buttercup said. "I bet that's where the monsters have their challenges."

The Girls flew to the stadium and landed in the center. A tall orange monster with bumpy, scaly skin and a spiked tail stood there with a pointy-toothed smile on his face.

"Buttercup, at last!" said the monster in a booming voice. "The crowd was starting to get anxious."

Buttercup looked around. The stands were filled with creepy monsters of all kinds.

"I am the toughest monster on Monster Isle. And I will prove it by defeating you, the toughest Powerpuff Girl!" Orgon cried.

"That's what you think," Buttercup shot back.

A loud bell rang, and Orgon stomped toward her. Buttercup remembered Calvin's tip. She flew to Orgon's right ear and started tickling.

But Orgon didn't start giggling, the way Buttercup's sisters did when she tickled them. "Is that how you fight? I thought you were supposed to be tough," he said, sounding angry.

Calvin had tricked her! *I should have known better*, Buttercup told herself. She became more determined than ever to win.

That determination showed in her battle. Orgon stomped and spit fire at her, but Buttercup responded in classic Powerpuff style. Within minutes, Orgon shouted, "I give up! You win!"

"I did it! I'm the toughest!" Buttercup cried.

The monsters in the stands did not like to see their toughest fighter defeated by a Powerpuff Girl. They began to boo and throw their signs. Blossom and Bubbles flew to Buttercup's side.

"These monsters are angry," Blossom said nervously. "And there are too many of them to fight!"

"Let's get out of here," Buttercup told her sisters.

Continue on page 64.

"These monsters look like trouble," Buttercup
said. "Let's see if they make the first move."

Buttercup didn't have to wait long. The monsters
opened their mouths and shot streams of flame at
the Girls.

"Hey, quit it!" Buttercup cried. She and her
sisters zoomed down to the monsters. They picked
up the monsters by their tails and started swinging
them around.

"We've got you now, you mean monsters!"
Bubbles said.

Suddenly, a deep voice startled them.

"STOP!"

Buttercup and her sisters paused. An orange monster came running around the corner. He looked a
lot like the blue and pink monsters, only bigger.

"Please stop, Powerpuff Girls," the orange monster pleaded.

"Why should we? Who are you?" Buttercup asked.

"I am Orgon," said the monster. "And these are my brother and sister, Orville and Olive."

"Orgon, The Powerpuff Girls are bothering us," whined Orville, the pink monster.

Buttercup let go of Orville's spiky tail, and he tumbled to the ground.

"You guys started it," Buttercup said. "So, Orgon, what do you say? I'm here to battle you, not your baby brother."

Orgon shook his head. "I wanted to prove that I was the toughest monster by defeating you," he said. "But seeing my little brother and sister fighting with you made me realize that fighting isn't always the best way to make your point. They could have gotten hurt, which is the last thing that I want. They're always getting into trouble trying to prove that *they're* tough, too, and I think I've been setting a bad example. Let's cancel the battle, okay?"

"No problem," Buttercup agreed. "I'm sure someone in Townsville needs our help, anyway."

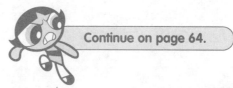

Continue on page 64.

The Powerpuff Girls streaked across the sky as they headed back to Townsville.

"Monster Isle was pretty amazing," Blossom remarked.

"Yeah, but I'm glad we're going back to Townsville," said Bubbles.

"Yeah," agreed Buttercup. "Monster Isle is an interesting place to visit, but I definitely wouldn't want to live there!"

So once again, the day is saved—not in Townsville, but on Monster Isle—thanks to The Powerpuff Girls!